by Mignonne Gunasekara
& Charis Mather

Minneapolis, Minnesota

Credits
Images are courtesy of Shutterstock.com. With thanks to Getty Images, Thinkstock Photo, and iStockphoto.
RECURRING – Amovitania. COVER – Bahau. 4–5 – Clement Kiragu, Gecko1968, Martijn. 6–7 – jindrich_pavelka, Erwin Niemand. 8–9 – JohanSwanepoel, Stu Porter, e2dan. 10–11 – Vladimir Wrangel, neelsky. 12–13 – Zhiltsov Alexandr, FloridaStock. 14–15 – Bildagentur Zoonar GmbH, Jim Cumming. 16–17 – Martin Mecnarowski, Konstantin39. 18–19 – Nagel Photography, Francois van Heerden. 20–21 – slowmotiongli, Subphoto.com. 22–23 – GR92100, Guillermo El Oso, Ondrej Prosicky. 24 – Francois van Heerden.

Bearport Publishing Company Product Development Team
President: Jen Jenson; Director of Product Development: Spencer Brinker; Managing Editor: Allison Juda; Associate Editor: Naomi Reich; Associate Editor: Tiana Tran; Art Director: Colin O'Dea; Designer: Elena Klinkner; Designer: Kayla Eggert; Product Development Assistant: Owen Hamlin

Library of Congress Cataloging-in-Publication Data is available at www.loc.gov or upon request from the publisher.

ISBN: 979-8-88916-575-0 (hardcover)
ISBN: 979-8-88916-580-4 (paperback)
ISBN: 979-8-88916-584-2 (ebook)

© 2024 BookLife Publishing
This edition is published by arrangement with BookLife Publishing.

North American adaptations © 2024 Bearport Publishing Company. All rights reserved. No part of this publication may be reproduced in whole or in part, stored in any retrieval system, or transmitted in any form or by any means, electronic, mechanical, photocopying, recording, or otherwise, without written permission from the publisher.

For more information, write to Bearport Publishing, 5357 Penn Avenue South, Minneapolis, MN 55419.

CONTENTS

Welcome to the World of Predators...4
Beastly Honey Badgers...6
Lethal Lions...8
Fierce Fishing Cats...10
Powerful Polar Bears...12
Wild Gray Wolves...14
Frightening Fossas...16
Dangerous African Wild Dogs...18
Outrageous Orcas...20
Mighty and Merciless...22
Glossary...24
Index...24

WELCOME TO THE WORLD OF PREDATORS

Many wild animals hunt other animals for food. These hunters are called predators.

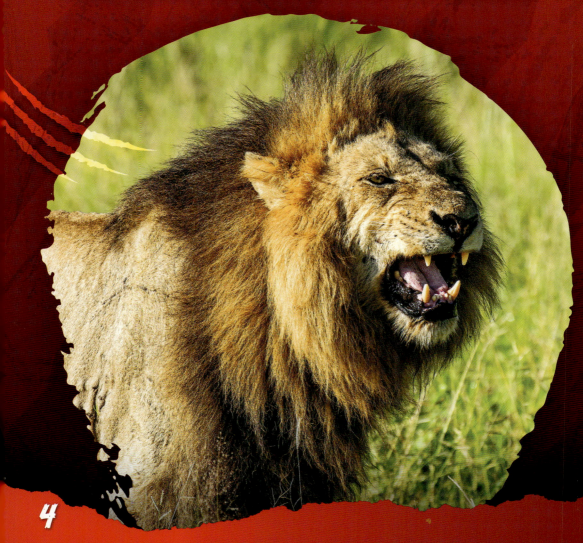

Some mammals are strong hunters. **Prey** does not stand a chance against these **warm-blooded** animals!

Get ready to meet mighty mammals.

BEASTLY HONEY BADGERS

Honey badgers are ready for a fight. They have thick skin.

These mighty mammals also have long claws.

They use their claws to break into beehives. Then, they eat the honey and bee **larvae** inside.

LETHAL LIONS

Lions live in family groups called prides.

A pride

The **female** lions of the **pride** usually do most of the hunting.

Sometimes, they hunt in groups.

They work together to take down animals bigger than themselves.

Fierce Fishing Cats

Fishing cats are great swimmers.

They hunt fish in the water.

These cats have two layers of fur in their coats.

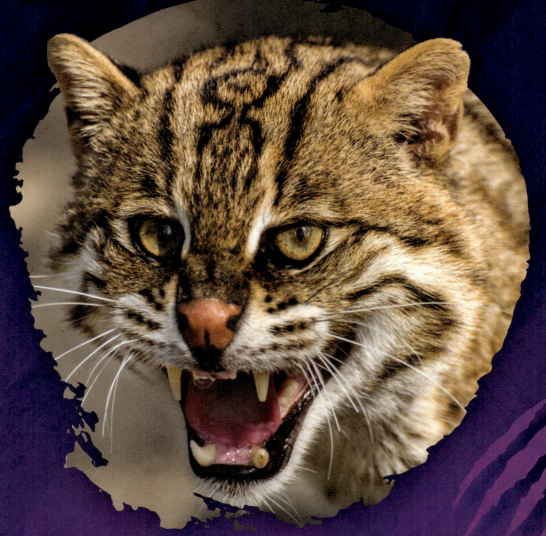

The extra layer helps stop water from reaching their skin as they find a meal.

POWERFUL Polar BEARS

Polar bears are the largest meat eaters on land.

They have big claws to help them hunt.

These huge mammals wait for prey near holes in the ice.

When seals pop up from the water, polar bears strike with their claws.

WILD GRAY WOLVES

Gray wolves hunt together in groups called packs.

A pack

They surround their prey. Then, the pack **attacks** from all sides.

Gray wolves travel far in search of food. Their speed helps them chase down any prey that tries to escape.

FRIGHTENING FOSSAS

Fossas are the largest **carnivores** in Madagascar (MAD-uh-gas-kahr).

Their tails are almost as long as their bodies.

They use them to keep themselves from falling as they hunt from the trees.

DANGEROUS AFRICAN WILD DOGS

Because of the patterns on their fur, African wild dogs are also called painted dogs.

They hunt together in packs.

Together, African wild dogs can take down large prey, such as wildebeests.

OUTRAGEOUS ORCAS

Orcas are powerful mammals that hunt in the ocean.

They are also known as killer whales.

These predators use **echolocation** (EK-oh-loh-KAY-shuhn) to find their prey. They make sounds and listen for the echoes.

Then, they attack.

MIGHTY AND MERCILESS

Mammals are everywhere in the world. They live on land and in the oceans.

Some hunt alone. Others work together to take down prey.

They are all mighty in their own way!

Glossary

attacks causes harm

carnivores animals that eat only meat

echolocation the process in which animals locate objects by sending out sounds and listening for their echoes

female an animal that can give birth or lay eggs

larvae young insects that have wormlike bodies

prey animals that are hunted for food

warm-blooded having blood that stays the same temperature no matter the temperature of the environment

Index

claws 6–7, 12–13
fur 11, 18
ice 13
land 12, 22
oceans 20, 22

packs 14, 18
prides 8
tails 17
water 10–11, 13